Mastering Fuse Glass Making

From Basics to Brilliant Artistry

Aaron Terry

copyright@2024

Table of Content

CHAPTER 1

Introduction to Fuse Glass Making

The History of Fuse Glass Making

What is Fused Glass?

Understanding the Art and Craft of Fused Glass

CHAPTER 2

Essential Tools and Materials

Types of Glass Used in Fusing

Essential Tools

Essential Materials

Safety Tools for Fused Glass Making

Safety Precautions for Fused Glass Making

CHAPTER 3

Getting Started: Basic Techniques

Basic Fused Glass Techniques

Intermediate Techniques

CHAPTER 4

Advanced Techniques

Kiln Operation and Maintenance

CHAPTER 5

Beginner Projects

Fused Glass Coasters

Fused Glass Pendant

Fused Glass Sun Catcher

Fused Glass Magnets

Fused Glass Dish

Fused Glass Wall Art

CHAPTER 6

Intermediate Projects

Fused Glass Bowl with Inclusions

Fused Glass Mosaic Panel

Fused Glass Vase

Fused Glass Wall Clock

CHAPTER 7

Advanced Projects

Fused Glass Sculpture

Fused Glass Installation

Fused Glass Mural

Fused Glass Functional Art Furniture

Fused Glass Sculptural Lighting Fixture

Fused Glass Architectural Feature

CHAPTER 8

Troubleshooting and Tips

General Tips

CONCLUSION

CHAPTER 1
Introduction to Fuse Glass Making

The History of Fuse Glass Making
Ancient Beginnings:

Origins in Mesopotamia (circa 2000 BCE): The earliest known fused glass artifacts were created by ancient Mesopotamians. These early craftsmen discovered that by heating glass fragments, they could fuse them into solid forms. These primitive techniques were used to create small items like beads and amulets.

Egyptian Contributions (circa 1500 BCE): The Egyptians advanced glass-making techniques, including the creation of glass tiles and inlays. Fused glass was often used in jewelry and decorative art, showcasing vibrant colors and intricate designs.

The Roman Empire:

Technological Advancements (circa 1st century BCE - 4th century CE): The Romans perfected many glass-making techniques, including glass blowing and fusing. They used these techniques to create a wide range of items, from functional vessels to decorative mosaics.

Glass Workshops: Roman glass workshops, particularly those in Alexandria, were renowned for their high-quality glass. The city became a major center for glass production and innovation.

Medieval and Renaissance Europe:

Decline and Revival (5th - 15th centuries): During the early medieval period, the art of glass fusing saw a decline due to the fall of the Roman Empire. However, it experienced a revival during the Renaissance as artisans rediscovered ancient techniques and incorporated them into new artistic expressions.

Stained Glass Windows (12th century onward): The use of fused glass in stained glass windows became prominent in cathedrals across Europe. Artisans created intricate designs by fusing colored glass pieces, adding a new dimension to religious and architectural art.

Modern Era:

Industrial Revolution (18th - 19th centuries): The advent of industrialization brought significant changes to glass production. Mass production techniques made glass more accessible, but traditional fused glass techniques became less common.

Studio Glass Movement (1960s - Present): The studio glass movement, which began in the 1960s, marked a resurgence of interest in glass as an art form. Artists like Harvey Littleton and Dominick Labino pioneered new techniques and emphasized the artistic potential of glass fusing.

Contemporary Innovations: Today, fuse glass making is a vibrant art form practiced by artisans worldwide. Modern kilns, tools, and materials have expanded the possibilities of what can be created, from intricate jewelry to large-scale installations.

Cultural Significance:

Symbolism and Rituals: Fused glass has been used in various cultural rituals and as symbols of status and wealth. For example, in ancient Egypt, fused glass was often associated with the divine and used in religious artifacts.

Art and Function: Throughout history, fused glass has served both artistic and functional purposes. Its versatility has made it a medium for artistic expression and practical applications in everyday life.

Key Historical Artifacts:

The Portland Vase (Roman, 1st century BCE): An exquisite example of Roman glass fusing, featuring intricate cameo work.

The Lycurgus Cup (Roman, 4th century CE): A stunning example of dichroic glass, changing color when viewed from different angles, showcasing advanced Roman techniques.

Medieval Stained Glass Windows: Examples like the windows of Chartres

Cathedral in France highlight the sophisticated use of fused glass in medieval art.

Influential Figures:

Louis Comfort Tiffany (1848-1933): An American artist renowned for his work with stained and fused glass, particularly his iconic Tiffany lamps.

Dale Chihuly (1941-): A contemporary glass artist known for his large-scale glass installations and innovative use of fused glass techniques.

What is Fused Glass?

Fused glass is a technique that involves the process of joining pieces of glass together by heating them in a kiln at high temperatures until they melt and fuse into a single piece. This method allows for the creation of intricate designs and patterns, as well as a variety of textures and shapes. Fused glass can be used for both decorative and functional items, ranging from jewelry and small art pieces to larger architectural elements like panels and tiles.

Understanding the Art and Craft of Fused Glass

Fused glass making is both an art and a craft that combines creativity with technical skill. It involves transforming raw glass materials into beautiful, functional, or decorative objects through the process of heating and fusing in a kiln. To fully appreciate and master this medium, one must understand both the artistic and technical aspects of the craft.

The Artistic Side of Fused Glass

Creativity and Expression:

Design and Composition: Creating fused glass art requires a strong sense of design and composition. Artists must think about how different pieces of glass will interact when fused, considering color, texture, and form.

Color Theory: Understanding color theory is crucial. Artists need to know how different colors of glass will look when fused together and how they can create harmonious or contrasting effects.

Inspiration and Themes: Like any art form, fused glass can be inspired by a variety of sources, including nature, abstract ideas, or personal experiences. Themes can range from organic and fluid designs to geometric and structured patterns.

Aesthetic Elements:

Transparency and Opacity: Glass comes in various degrees of transparency and opacity. Combining these elements can create depth and dimension in the artwork.

Light Interaction: Fused glass has a unique relationship with light. The way light passes through, reflects off, and interacts with the glass can significantly impact the final piece. Artists often experiment with light to enhance their work.

Textures and Layers: By layering different types of glass and using various fusing techniques, artists can create interesting textures and layered effects that add complexity to their pieces.

CHAPTER 2
Essential Tools and Materials

Types of Glass Used in Fusing

Fused glass making requires specific types of glass that are compatible in terms of their thermal properties to ensure successful fusion without cracking or other issues. The most important characteristic to consider is the coefficient of expansion (COE), which measures how much the glass expands and contracts when heated and cooled. Here are the main types of glass used in fusing:

Bullseye Glass (COE 90)

- Description: Bullseye glass is one of the most popular and widely used types of glass for fusing. It is manufactured by Bullseye Glass Company and has a COE of 90.
- Variety: It comes in a wide range of colors, transparencies, and textures. Bullseye glass also includes specialty glasses like iridescent, dichroic, and patterned glass.
- Applications: Ideal for both beginners and advanced artists, Bullseye glass is used in a variety of projects, from

small jewelry pieces to large panels and sculptures.

Spectrum System 96 (COE 96)

- Description: Spectrum System 96 glass is another popular choice for glass fusing. It was originally produced by Spectrum Glass Company and is now made by Oceanside Glass & Tile. It has a COE of 96.
- Variety: This glass is available in a wide range of colors and styles, including transparent, opalescent, and iridescent varieties.
- Applications: Suitable for all levels of artists, Spectrum System 96 glass is commonly used in fusing projects like functional ware, decorative items, and art pieces.

Float Glass (COE Varies)

- Description: Float glass, also known as window glass, is a type of glass made by floating molten glass on a bed of molten metal. Its COE can vary, but it is generally around 84-86.

- Variety: It is typically clear, but can be found in different colors and thicknesses.
- Applications: Float glass is often used for experimental or large-scale projects due to its availability and low cost. However, it is less commonly used for precise artistic work due to its variability in COE.

Dichroic Glass (COE 90 or 96)

- Description: Dichroic glass is coated with a thin film of metal oxides, giving it a reflective and iridescent appearance. It is available in both COE 90 and COE 96 to match Bullseye and Spectrum glass.
- Variety: It comes in a variety of colors and patterns, including textured and smooth surfaces.
- Applications: Dichroic glass is highly prized for its shimmering effects and is often used in jewelry, decorative accents, and focal points in fused glass art.

Borofloat Glass (COE 33)

- Description: Borofloat glass, also known as borosilicate glass, has a

COE of 33. It is known for its high resistance to thermal shock and is used in scientific and industrial applications.

- Variety: Typically clear, but can be colored through various processes.
- Applications: While not commonly used in traditional fused glass art, it is used in specialized applications where durability and thermal resistance are crucial.

Specialty Glasses

- Iridescent Glass: This glass has a metallic coating that gives it a rainbow-like appearance. It can be used to add special effects and visual interest to fused glass projects.
- Reactive Glass: Certain types of glass react with each other during the fusing process to create unique colors and patterns. For example, combining copper-bearing and sulfur-bearing glasses can produce interesting effects.
- Confetti Glass: Small, thin pieces of glass that can be sprinkled over a project to add color and texture.

- Frit: Ground glass available in various sizes (coarse to powder) used to add texture and color to fused glass pieces.

Essential Tools

Glass Cutters:

- Description: Glass cutters have a small, sharp wheel designed to score the surface of the glass, making it easier to snap along the scored line.
- Types: Standard hand-held cutters and pistol-grip cutters, which provide additional leverage and comfort.

Running Pliers:

- Description: These pliers help break the glass along the scored line. They have a curved jaw that applies pressure on both sides of the score to ensure a clean break.

Grozing Pliers:

- Description: Used for nibbling away small pieces of glass to refine the edges after cutting. They feature serrated jaws that firmly grip the glass.

Glass Grinders:

- Description: Electric grinders with diamond-coated bits used to smooth and shape the edges of cut glass pieces. Essential for achieving precise fits and smooth edges.

Kiln:

- Description: A special oven designed to reach high temperatures necessary for fusing glass. Kilns come in various sizes and shapes, from small tabletop models to larger, floor-standing units.
- Features: Look for a kiln with a digital controller for precise temperature control and programmable firing schedules.

Kiln Shelf:

- Description: A heat-resistant shelf that holds the glass pieces inside the kiln. Shelves need to be coated with kiln wash to prevent glass from sticking.

Kiln Wash or Shelf Primer:

- Description: A protective coating applied to the kiln shelf to prevent glass from sticking during the firing process.

Fusing Molds:

- Description: Ceramic or stainless steel molds used to shape glass pieces during the slumping process. They come in various shapes, including bowls, plates, and more intricate forms.

Cutting Mats and Rulers:

- Description: Heat-resistant mats provide a safe surface for cutting glass. Metal rulers are used to measure and guide cuts accurately.

Safety Gear:

- Safety Glasses: Protect your eyes from glass shards and dust.
- Gloves: Wear cut-resistant gloves when handling glass.
- Dust Mask: Use when grinding glass or working with fine glass powders and frit.

Essential Materials

Glass:

- Types: Bullseye (COE 90), Spectrum System 96 (COE 96), Dichroic glass, and specialty glasses like iridescent and reactive glass.
- Forms: Sheet glass, frit (ground glass), stringers (thin rods), confetti glass, and millefiori (decorative glass pieces).

Adhesives:

- Glue: Clear, water-soluble glue to temporarily hold glass pieces in place before firing.

Kiln Paper: Thin paper that acts as a barrier between the glass and the kiln shelf, preventing sticking and making cleanup easier.

Glass Cleaner: Used to clean glass pieces before fusing to ensure no dust or oils interfere with the fusing process.

Copper Foil and Wire: Used for creating embedded designs or structures within fused glass pieces.

Nippers and Snappers: Hand tools used for cutting small pieces of glass or trimming glass rods and stringers.

Additional Tools and Accessories

Rods and Stringers: Thin rods of glass that can be used to add linear designs or structural elements to fused glass projects.

Frit Sifters: Tools for sorting frit by size to create different textural effects.

Bead Racks and Mandrels: Used for creating glass beads, these racks hold mandrels (metal rods) coated with bead release to prevent glass from sticking.

Glass Nibbler: A hand tool used for nibbling away small sections of glass to refine shapes and edges.

Thermocouples: Temperature sensors used in kilns to accurately measure and control the firing temperature.

Cleaning and Maintenance Tools

Brushes: Used for applying kiln wash to shelves and molds.

Scrapers: Used to remove kiln wash from shelves and molds after firing.

Vacuum Cleaner: A small, handheld vacuum can help clean up glass dust and debris from your workspace.

Safety Tools for Fused Glass Making

Working with glass and high temperatures in fused glass making requires careful attention to safety. Proper safety tools and practices are essential to prevent injuries and ensure a safe working environment. Below is a comprehensive list of safety tools you should have:

Safety Glasses or Goggles:

- Description: Protect your eyes from glass shards, dust, and other debris.
- Features: Look for glasses or goggles with side shields for extra protection.

Cut-Resistant Gloves:

- Description: Protect your hands from cuts when handling glass.
- Types: Kevlar or other cut-resistant materials are recommended.

Dust Masks or Respirators:

- Description: Protect your lungs from inhaling fine glass particles, powders, and fumes.
- Types: N95 masks are suitable for general protection; respirators with appropriate filters may be necessary for more hazardous materials.

Heat-Resistant Gloves:

- Description: Protect your hands from burns when handling hot items and working near the kiln.
- Features: Ensure they are rated for high temperatures and provide good dexterity.

Aprons:

- Description: Protect your clothing and skin from glass shards and chemicals.
- Types: Heavy-duty fabric or leather aprons are ideal.

First Aid Kit:

- Description: Essential for treating minor cuts, burns, and other injuries.
- Contents: Should include adhesive bandages, antiseptic wipes, sterile gauze pads, burn cream, tweezers, and scissors.

Fire Extinguisher:

- Description: Essential for quickly extinguishing small fires.
- Types: A Class C (electrical) fire extinguisher is recommended for kiln areas.

Ventilation System:

- Description: Proper ventilation is necessary to remove fumes and airborne particles from the workspace.
- Types: Fume hoods or exhaust fans are recommended to ensure adequate air circulation.

Cutting Mats:

- Description: Provide a safe, stable surface for cutting glass.
- Features: Heat-resistant and durable to withstand repeated use.

Bench Brushes and Dust Pans:

- Description: Used to clean up glass shards and dust from work surfaces.
- Types: Soft-bristled brushes are ideal to avoid scattering glass fragments.

Vacuum Cleaner:

- Description: A small, handheld vacuum can help clean up glass dust and debris from your workspace.
- Features: A vacuum with HEPA filter is ideal for capturing fine particles.

Kiln Safety Tools:

- Kiln Gloves: Specifically designed to handle high temperatures when loading and unloading the kiln.
- Kiln Tongs: Long-handled tongs for handling hot items inside the kiln.
- Kiln Ventilation System: Ensures that fumes are safely vented out of the workspace.

Lighting:

- Description: Good lighting is essential for precision work and to avoid accidents.
- Features: Bright, adjustable lights are recommended to illuminate the workspace effectively.

Safe Storage Solutions:

- Glass Storage Racks: Organize and store glass sheets safely to prevent breakage and accidents.
- Tool Storage: Keep tools organized and easily accessible to maintain a tidy and safe workspace.

Safety Precautions for Fused Glass Making

Ensuring safety while working with fused glass involves not only using the right tools and materials but also following important safety precautions.

Personal Safety

Wear Protective Gear:

Safety Glasses or Goggles: Always wear safety glasses or goggles to protect your eyes from flying glass shards and dust.

Cut-Resistant Gloves: Use cut-resistant gloves when handling and cutting glass to prevent cuts and injuries.

Dust Masks or Respirators: Wear a dust mask or respirator, especially when grinding glass or working with fine powders, to avoid inhaling harmful particles.

Heat-Resistant Gloves: Use heat-resistant gloves when handling hot items and working near the kiln to protect your hands from burns.

Aprons: Wear a heavy-duty apron to protect your clothing and skin from glass shards and chemicals.

Proper Handling Techniques

Handle glass carefully and always assume it could break.

Avoid using excessive force when cutting or breaking glass.

Always cut away from your body and keep your hands clear of the cutting path.

Safe Attire:

Wear long sleeves and pants to protect your skin from glass cuts.

Avoid loose clothing, and tie back long hair to prevent it from getting caught in equipment.

Workspace Safety

Organized Workspace:

Maintain a clean and uncluttered workspace to minimize the risk of accidents.

Store glass sheets vertically in a stable rack to prevent them from falling and breaking.

Proper Ventilation:

Ensure your workspace is well-ventilated to avoid inhaling fumes from adhesives, cleaners, and the kiln.

Use a fume hood or exhaust fan to improve air circulation, especially when working with chemicals or firing the kiln.

Kiln Safety:

Follow the manufacturer's instructions for operating and maintaining your kiln.

Never leave the kiln unattended while it is in use.

Place the kiln on a heat-resistant surface and ensure it is away from flammable materials.

Use kiln gloves and tongs when loading and unloading the kiln.

Ensure the kiln area is well-ventilated to avoid buildup of fumes.

Emergency Preparedness:

Keep a fire extinguisher rated for electrical fires (Class C) accessible in your workspace.

Familiarize yourself with emergency procedures and keep emergency contact numbers handy.

Ensure you have a well-stocked first aid kit available and know how to use it.

Chemical Safety

Proper Storage and Handling:

Store chemicals, including adhesives and cleaners, in their original containers and in a cool, dry place.

Follow all safety instructions and labels on chemical products.

Use chemicals only in well-ventilated areas to prevent inhaling fumes.

Avoid Contamination:

Clean your tools and workspace after using chemicals to avoid cross-contamination.

Do not eat, drink, or smoke in your workspace to prevent ingesting harmful substances.

Electrical Safety

Safe Equipment Use:

Regularly inspect electrical equipment, such as grinders and kilns, for damage or wear.

Do not overload electrical outlets and ensure that all cords are in good condition.

Turn off and unplug equipment when it's not in use.

Grounding:

Make sure all electrical equipment is properly grounded to prevent electrical shocks.

General Safety Tips

Proper Lighting: Ensure your workspace is well-lit to avoid accidents and ensure precision in your work.

Ergonomics: Set up your workspace to reduce strain on your body. Use comfortable, supportive seating and work at a height that prevents hunching or awkward postures.

Continuous Learning: Stay informed about the latest safety practices and techniques in fused glass making.

Attend workshops, read guides, and follow safety recommendations from trusted sources.

CHAPTER 3
Getting Started: Basic Techniques

Basic Fused Glass Techniques

Fused glass making involves a variety of techniques, but two fundamental methods are full fusing and tack fusing. These techniques form the foundation for many fused glass projects and are essential for beginners to master.

Full Fusing

Full fusing is the process of heating glass pieces in a kiln until they melt and fuse together into a smooth, uniform surface. This technique is ideal for creating flat glass pieces, such as tiles, coasters, and jewelry.

Materials and Tools Needed:

- Sheet glass (compatible COE)
- Glass cutter
- Running pliers
- Glass grinder (optional)
- Kiln and kiln shelf
- Kiln wash or kiln paper
- Safety gear (glasses, gloves, mask)

Steps:

Design Your Project: Sketch your design on paper to plan the arrangement and colors of the glass pieces.

Prepare the Glass: Clean the glass sheets with a glass cleaner to remove any dust or oils.

Use a glass cutter to score the glass according to your design.

Break the glass along the scored lines using running pliers.

Smooth any rough edges with a glass grinder if needed.

Arrange the Glass: Apply kiln wash to the kiln shelf or place a sheet of kiln paper to prevent the glass from sticking.

Arrange your cut glass pieces on the prepared kiln shelf. Ensure the pieces are evenly spaced and not too close to the edges of the shelf.

Prepare the Kiln: Place the kiln shelf with the arranged glass into the kiln.

Program the kiln with a full fusing schedule. A typical schedule might be:

Ramp 1: 300°F (150°C) per hour to 1100°F (593°C), hold for 10 minutes.

Ramp 2: 600°F (316°C) per hour to 1480°F (804°C), hold for 10 minutes.

Ramp 3: Full speed to 950°F (510°C), hold for 60 minutes.

Ramp 4: 100°F (56°C) per hour to 700°F (371°C), then off.

Fire the Kiln: Start the kiln and monitor the temperature to ensure it follows the programmed schedule.

Allow the kiln to cool completely before opening it to avoid thermal shock.

Finishing: Once the kiln has cooled to room temperature, carefully remove the fused glass piece.

Clean the piece to remove any residual kiln wash or kiln paper.

Tack Fusing

Tack fusing involves heating glass pieces just enough so they adhere to each other while retaining their individual shapes and textures. This technique is used for creating raised, textured designs.

Materials and Tools Needed:

- Sheet glass (compatible COE)
- Glass cutter
- Running pliers
- Glass grinder (optional)
- Kiln and kiln shelf
- Kiln wash or kiln paper
- Safety gear (glasses, gloves, mask)

Steps:

Design Your Project: Sketch your design on paper to plan the arrangement and colors of the glass pieces.

Prepare the Glass: Clean the glass sheets with a glass cleaner to remove any dust or oils.

Use a glass cutter to score the glass according to your design.

Break the glass along the scored lines using running pliers.

Smooth any rough edges with a glass grinder if needed.

Arrange the Glass: Apply kiln wash to the kiln shelf or place a sheet of kiln paper to prevent the glass from sticking.

Arrange your cut glass pieces on the prepared kiln shelf, layering them to create a textured design.

Prepare the Kiln: Place the kiln shelf with the arranged glass into the kiln.

Program the kiln with a tack fusing schedule. A typical schedule might be:

Ramp 1: 300°F (150°C) per hour to 1100°F (593°C), hold for 10 minutes.

Ramp 2: 600°F (316°C) per hour to 1350°F (732°C), hold for 10 minutes.

Ramp 3: Full speed to 950°F (510°C), hold for 60 minutes.

Ramp 4: 100°F (56°C) per hour to 700°F (371°C), then off.

Fire the Kiln: Start the kiln and monitor the temperature to ensure it follows the programmed schedule.

Allow the kiln to cool completely before opening it to avoid thermal shock.

Finishing: Once the kiln has cooled to room temperature, carefully remove the tack-fused glass piece.

Clean the piece to remove any residual kiln wash or kiln paper.

Slumping

Slumping is the process of heating a flat glass piece until it softens and slumps into or over a mold, creating a three-dimensional form. This technique is commonly used to make bowls, plates, and other curved glass objects.

Materials and Tools Needed:

- Glass piece (already fused or flat)
- Slumping mold
- Kiln and kiln shelf
- Kiln wash or kiln paper
- Safety gear (glasses, gloves, mask)

Steps:

Choose a Slumping Mold: Select a slumping mold that matches the desired shape and size of your finished piece. Slumping molds come in various shapes and materials, such as ceramic or stainless steel.

Prepare the Glass: If you're starting with a flat glass piece, ensure it has been properly fused and annealed.

Clean the glass piece with a glass cleaner to remove any dust or oils.

Prepare the Kiln: Apply kiln wash to the slumping mold or place a sheet of kiln paper on it to prevent the glass from sticking.

Place the prepared mold on the kiln shelf inside the kiln.

Position the Glass: Carefully place the glass piece on top of the slumping mold, ensuring it is centered and aligned with the mold's shape.

Program the Kiln: Program the kiln with a slumping schedule appropriate for the type and thickness of the glass. A typical schedule might be:

Ramp 1: 300°F (150°C) per hour to 1100°F (593°C), hold for 10 minutes.

Ramp 2: Full speed to slumping temperature (varies depending on glass thickness and desired slump depth), hold for appropriate time based on the glass thickness.

Ramp 3: 100°F (56°C) per hour to annealing temperature (usually around 900°F or 482°C), hold for 10 minutes.

Ramp 4: Anneal cool at 100°F (56°C) per hour to room temperature, then off.

Fire the Kiln: Start the kiln and monitor the temperature to ensure it follows the programmed schedule.

Allow the kiln to cool completely before opening it to avoid thermal shock.

Finishing: Once the kiln has cooled to room temperature, carefully remove the slumped glass piece from the mold.

Clean the piece to remove any residual kiln wash or kiln paper.

Glass Combing

Glass combing is a technique that involves pulling or combing molten glass to create intricate patterns and designs. This method produces unique and visually stunning results that can be incorporated into fused glass artwork.

Materials and Tools Needed:

- Sheet glass (compatible COE)
- Kiln and kiln shelf
- Kiln wash or kiln paper
- Stainless steel combing tool or rake

- Safety gear (glasses, gloves, mask)

Steps:

Prepare the Glass: Clean the glass sheets with a glass cleaner to remove any dust or oils.

Cut or arrange the glass pieces as desired for your design.

Prepare the Kiln: Apply kiln wash to the kiln shelf or place a sheet of kiln paper on it to prevent the glass from sticking.

Arrange the Glass: Arrange your glass pieces on the prepared kiln shelf, ensuring they are evenly spaced and not too close to the edges of the shelf.

Heat the Kiln: Program the kiln with a firing schedule appropriate for glass combing. This typically involves heating the kiln to a temperature where the glass becomes molten but does not fully fuse.

A typical schedule might include a gradual ramp to a temperature between 1600°F to 1700°F (871°C to 927°C), depending on the desired viscosity of the glass.

Apply Combing Technique: When the glass reaches the desired temperature, carefully use a stainless steel combing tool or rake to create patterns and designs in the molten glass.

Experiment with different combing techniques, such as dragging, swirling, or zigzagging, to achieve various effects.

Controlled Cooling: After applying the combing technique, allow the glass to cool slowly in the kiln to anneal and stabilize the piece.

Program the kiln to gradually reduce the temperature at a controlled rate to prevent thermal shock.

Finishing: Once the kiln has cooled to room temperature, carefully remove the glass piece.

Clean the piece to remove any residual kiln wash or kiln paper.

Intermediate Techniques

Glass Painting

Glass painting involves applying specialized glass paints or enamels onto the surface of glass pieces to create intricate designs, patterns, or imagery. This technique adds color and detail to fused glass artwork and allows for endless creative possibilities.

Materials and Tools Needed:

- Glass pieces (compatible COE)
- Glass paints or enamels
- Paint brushes (various sizes)
- Palette or mixing dishes
- Glass cleaner
- Kiln and kiln shelf
- Kiln wash or kiln paper
- Safety gear (glasses, gloves, mask)

Steps:

Prepare the Glass: Clean the glass pieces with a glass cleaner to remove any dust or oils. Ensure the glass is completely dry before painting.

Choose Your Design: Sketch your design on paper or plan it out beforehand. Consider the colors and techniques you want to use for your painting.

Mix Paints (If Necessary): If using powdered enamels, mix them with a medium to create a paintable consistency.Adhere to the manufacturer's instructions for mixing ratios.

Painting the Glass: Using a fine-tipped paintbrush, carefully apply the glass paints or enamels onto the surface of the glass. You can layer colors, blend them, or use different brush techniques to achieve various effects.

Let each layer of paint dry completely before adding additional layers or details.

Firing the Glass: Once your painting is complete and dry, place the glass piece on a kiln shelf lined with kiln wash or kiln paper.

Program the kiln with a firing schedule suitable for glass painting. This typically involves a ramp-up to the appropriate temperature for the paint to fuse with the glass, followed by an annealing cycle.

Follow the manufacturer's instructions for firing temperatures and schedules based on the specific paints or enamels you're using.

Cooling and Finishing: Allow the kiln to cool to room temperature before removing the painted glass piece.

Clean the piece to remove any residue or kiln wash marks. Your painted glass piece is now ready for display or further finishing.

Glass Layering

Glass layering involves stacking multiple layers of glass to create depth, dimension, and visual interest in fused glass artwork. This technique allows artists to incorporate various colors, textures, and effects into their designs.

Materials and Tools Needed:

- Sheet glass (compatible COE)
- Glass cutter
- Running pliers
- Glass grinder (optional)
- Kiln and kiln shelf
- Kiln wash or kiln paper
- Safety gear (glasses, gloves, mask)

Steps:

Design Your Project: Plan your design, considering the layers of glass you'll be stacking and the effects you want to achieve. Sketching or creating a blueprint can help visualize the final piece.

Prepare the Glass: Clean the glass sheets with a glass cleaner to remove any dust or oils.

Use a glass cutter to score the glass according to your design. You may need multiple layers of glass for each component of your design.

Cut and Arrange Glass Layers: Break the glass along the scored lines using running pliers.

Arrange the cut glass pieces into layers, stacking them according to your design plan. You can experiment with different colors, opacities, and textures to create depth and visual interest.

Stacking and Assembly: Apply kiln wash to the kiln shelf or place a sheet of kiln paper on it to prevent the glass from sticking.

Carefully stack the glass layers on the prepared kiln shelf, ensuring they are aligned and spaced appropriately.

Firing the Kiln: Program the kiln with a firing schedule suitable for glass layering. This typically involves a ramp-up to the appropriate temperature for full fusing, followed by an annealing cycle.

Follow the manufacturer's instructions for firing temperatures and schedules based on the specific types and thicknesses of glass you're using.

Cooling and Finishing: Allow the kiln to cool to room temperature before removing the fused glass piece.

Clean the piece to remove any residue or kiln wash marks. Your layered glass artwork is now ready for display or further finishing.

Glass Slurry Casting

Glass slurry casting involves creating a mold from a refractory material and filling it with a slurry mixture of powdered glass and a binder. This technique allows for the creation of intricate and detailed glass sculptures with smooth surfaces.

Materials and Tools Needed:
- Refractory mold material (such as plaster or ceramic)
- Powdered glass (compatible COE)
- Binder (such as gum arabic or PVA glue)
- Mixing container and stirring utensil
- Kiln and kiln shelf
- Safety gear (glasses, gloves, mask)

Steps:

Prepare the Mold: Create or obtain a mold made from a refractory material, such as plaster or ceramic. Make sure the mold is clean and dry before use.

Mix the Slurry: In a mixing container, combine powdered glass with a binder, such as gum arabic or PVA glue. The consistency should be similar to pancake batter.

Fill the Mold: Pour the slurry mixture into the prepared mold, ensuring it fills all the intricate details of the mold.

Remove Air Bubbles: Tap the mold gently on a flat surface to release any air bubbles trapped in the slurry mixture.

Dry the Casting: Allow the slurry casting to dry completely in the mold. This may take several hours or overnight, depending on the size and thickness of the casting.

Fire the Kiln: Once the casting is dry, carefully remove it from the mold and place it on a kiln shelf.

Program the kiln with a firing schedule suitable for slurry casting, including a ramp-up to the appropriate temperature for full fusing and annealing.

Cooling and Finishing: Allow the kiln to cool to room temperature before removing the fused glass casting.

Clean the piece to remove any residue or kiln wash marks. Your slurry cast glass sculpture is now ready for display or further finishing.

Glass Combing with Inclusions

Glass combing with inclusions is a variation of the glass combing technique that involves embedding additional materials, such as metal wires, foils, or stringers, into the molten glass to create unique patterns and textures.

Materials and Tools Needed:

- Sheet glass (compatible COE)
- Kiln and kiln shelf
- Kiln wash or kiln paper
- Stainless steel combing tool or rake
- Inclusion materials (such as metal wires, foils, or stringers)
- Safety gear (glasses, gloves, mask)

Steps:

Prepare the Glass: Clean the glass sheets with a glass cleaner to remove any dust or oils.

Prepare the Inclusion Materials: Cut or prepare the inclusion materials, such as metal wires, foils, or stringers, to the desired length and shape.

Arrange the Glass Layers: Stack multiple layers of glass on a kiln shelf, alternating colors and textures as desired.

Add Inclusion Materials: Place the prepared inclusion materials onto the top layer of glass, arranging them in the desired pattern or design.

Heat the Kiln: Program the kiln with a firing schedule suitable for glass combing with inclusions. This typically involves a gradual ramp-up to the appropriate temperature for full fusing, followed by an annealing cycle.

Apply Combing Technique: When the glass reaches the desired temperature, carefully use a stainless steel combing tool or rake to create patterns and designs in the molten glass, incorporating the inclusion materials into the design.

Controlled Cooling: After applying the combing technique, allow the glass to cool slowly in the kiln to anneal and stabilize the piece.

Program the kiln to gradually reduce the temperature at a controlled rate to prevent thermal shock.

Finishing: Once the kiln has cooled to room temperature, carefully remove the glass piece.

Clean the piece to remove any residue or kiln wash marks. Your glass combing with inclusions artwork is now ready for display or further finishing.

CHAPTER 4
Advanced Techniques

Glass Casting with Lost Wax

Glass casting with lost wax is a complex technique that involves creating intricate glass sculptures by first making a wax model, then creating a mold around the model, melting out the wax, and finally casting glass into the empty mold cavity. This technique allows for the creation of detailed and highly sculptural glass pieces.

Materials and Tools Needed:

- Sculpting wax
- Sculpting tools
- Investment material (such as plaster-silica or ceramic shell)
- Kiln and kiln shelf
- Glass frit or billets
- Safety gear (glasses, gloves, mask)

Steps:

Create a Wax Model: Sculpt your desired design using sculpting wax and sculpting tools. The wax model should be the exact size and shape of the final glass sculpture.

Prepare the Mold: Create a mold around the wax model using investment material, such as plaster-silica or ceramic shell. Allow the mold to fully cure and harden.

Remove the Wax: Heat the mold in a kiln to melt out the wax from the mold cavity, leaving behind an empty space in the shape of the wax model.

Prepare the Glass: Heat glass frit or billets in a kiln until they are molten and fluid.

Pour the Glass: Carefully pour the molten glass into the empty mold cavity, filling it completely.

Cooling and Demolding: Allow the glass to cool and solidify inside the mold.

Once cooled, carefully break away the investment material to reveal the cast glass sculpture.

Finishing: Clean and polish the cast glass sculpture as needed to remove any rough edges or imperfections.

Your glass casting with lost wax sculpture is now ready for display or further finishing.

Pâte de Verre

Pâte de verre is a traditional glassworking technique that involves creating glass objects by packing layers of glass frit or powder into a mold and firing them in a kiln. This technique allows for the creation of intricate, translucent glass pieces with delicate detail and color variation.

Materials and Tools Needed:

- Glass frit or powder (compatible COE)
- Molds (made of refractory material, such as plaster-silica)
- Kiln and kiln shelf
- Safety gear (glasses, gloves, mask)

Steps:

Prepare the Mold: Choose or create a mold with the desired shape and size for your pâte de verre piece. Molds are typically made of refractory material, such as plaster-silica.

Prepare the Glass: Select glass frit or powder in the desired colors and sizes. Mix different colors and opacities to create unique effects.

Fill the Mold: Layer the glass frit or powder into the mold, using a variety of colors and opacities to create depth and dimension. Pack the glass tightly into the mold to ensure a solid structure.

Fire the Kiln: Program the kiln with a firing schedule suitable for pâte de verre. This typically involves a gradual ramp-up to the appropriate temperature for full fusing and annealing.

Cooling and Demolding: Allow the kiln to cool to room temperature before removing the pâte de verre piece from the mold.

Carefully demold the piece, taking care not to damage the delicate glass structure.

Finishing: Clean and polish the pâte de verre piece as needed to enhance its clarity and translucency.

Your pâte de verre glass piece is now ready for display or further finishing.

Glass Powder Printing

Glass powder printing is a technique that involves applying layers of finely ground glass powders onto a glass surface to create detailed images or designs. This technique allows for precise control over color and texture, resulting in intricate and visually stunning fused glass artwork.

Materials and Tools Needed:

- Sheet glass (compatible COE)
- Glass powders (various colors)
- Paint brushes (various sizes)
- Stencils or silk screens (optional)
- Sifting tools (such as sieves or screens)
- Kiln and kiln shelf
- Safety gear (glasses, gloves, mask)

Steps:

Prepare the Glass: Clean the glass sheet with a glass cleaner to remove any dust or oils.

Apply Glass Powders: Using a paintbrush or sifting tool, apply layers of finely ground glass powders onto the glass surface. You can create intricate designs freehand or use stencils or silk screens for more precise patterns.

Layering and Detailing: Experiment with layering different colors and opacities of glass powders to create depth and dimension in your design. Use finer powders for intricate details and coarser powders for larger areas of color.

Firing the Kiln: Place the glass sheet with the applied powders onto a kiln shelf.

Program the kiln with a firing schedule suitable for glass powder printing, including a ramp-up to the appropriate temperature for full fusing and annealing.

Cooling and Finishing: Allow the kiln to cool to room temperature before removing the fused glass piece.

Clean the piece to remove any residue or kiln wash marks. Your glass powder printed artwork is now ready for display or further finishing.

Kiln Carving

Kiln carving is a technique that involves creating relief or texture on a glass surface by carving away portions of the glass before firing it in a kiln. This technique adds depth and dimension to fused glass artwork and allows for the creation of intricate patterns and designs.

Materials and Tools Needed:

- Sheet glass (compatible COE)
- Carving tools (such as diamond bits or abrasive wheels)
- Kiln and kiln shelf
- Safety gear (glasses, gloves, mask)

Steps:

Design Your Carving: Plan your design, considering the areas you want to carve away and the desired depth and texture of the carving.

Prepare the Glass: Clean the glass sheet with a glass cleaner to remove any dust or oils.

Carve the Glass: Using carving tools, carefully carve away portions of the glass surface to create your desired design. You can create relief, texture, or intricate patterns depending on your artistic vision.

Firing the Kiln: Place the carved glass piece onto a kiln shelf.

Program the kiln with a firing schedule suitable for kiln carving, including a ramp-up to the appropriate temperature for full fusing and annealing.

Cooling and Finishing: Allow the kiln to cool to room temperature before removing the fused glass piece.

Clean the piece to remove any residue or kiln wash marks. Your kiln carved glass artwork is now ready for display or further finishing.

Kiln Operation and Maintenance

Operating and maintaining a kiln is essential for ensuring the safety and functionality of the equipment, as well as achieving consistent and successful results in fused glass making.

Kiln Operation

Preparation:

- Ensure the kiln is placed on a level, stable surface, away from flammable materials and with proper ventilation.
- Check that all electrical connections are secure and the kiln is plugged into a dedicated outlet with the appropriate voltage and amperage.

Loading:

- Arrange glass pieces on kiln shelves, ensuring proper spacing and avoiding contact between pieces.
- Use kiln posts or furniture to create layers and prevent glass from sticking to shelves during firing.

Programming:

- Program the kiln controller with the appropriate firing schedule for the specific technique and glass being used.
- Ensure the ramp rates, hold times, and target temperatures are set according to manufacturer recommendations or established best practices.

Firing:

- Start the firing cycle and monitor the kiln throughout the process, especially during temperature ramp-ups and holds.
- Observe the kiln through peepholes or viewports to check for any issues, such as uneven heating or devitrification.

Cooling:

- After the firing cycle is complete, allow the kiln to cool gradually to room temperature to prevent thermal shock and stress on the glass.
- Avoid opening the kiln door too soon to prevent rapid cooling, which can cause cracking or breakage of the glass.

Kiln Maintenance

Cleaning:

- Regularly clean the kiln interior, shelves, and elements to remove dust, debris, and glass residue that can affect firing results.
- Use a soft brush or vacuum to remove loose particles, and wipe surfaces with a damp cloth or mild cleaner.

Element Inspection:

- Check kiln elements for signs of wear, damage, or deterioration, such as hot spots, breaks, or sagging.

- Replace damaged or worn elements promptly to maintain even heating and prevent kiln malfunction.

Ventilation:

- Ensure adequate ventilation around the kiln to remove fumes, gases, and heat generated during firing.
- Install a vent hood or exhaust system if necessary to improve air circulation and maintain a safe working environment.

Safety Checks:

- Regularly inspect kiln components, such as thermocouples, relays, and controllers, for proper functioning and calibration.
- Test emergency shut-off systems and fire safety equipment to ensure they are in working order.

Kiln Furniture:

- Inspect kiln shelves, posts, and other furniture for cracks, warping, or damage that could affect firing results.

- Replace worn or damaged furniture as needed to maintain proper kiln stacking and support.

CHAPTER 5
Beginner Projects

Fused Glass Coasters

Materials Needed:

- Sheet glass (compatible COE)
- Glass cutter
- Running pliers
- Kiln and kiln shelf
- Kiln wash or kiln paper
- Safety gear (glasses, gloves, mask)
- Optional: Glass frit, stringers, or decals for decoration

Steps:

Design: Decide on the shape and size of your coasters. Simple shapes like squares or circles are ideal for beginners.

Prepare Glass: Cut your sheet glass into coaster-sized pieces using a glass cutter. You can also experiment with layering different colors or adding decorative elements like frit or stringers.

Arrange on Kiln Shelf: Apply kiln wash to the kiln shelf or use kiln paper to prevent glass from sticking. Arrange your glass pieces on the shelf, leaving a small gap between each piece.

Fire Kiln: Program your kiln with a full fusing schedule suitable for the thickness of your glass. Typically, this involves ramping up to a temperature between 1450°F to 1550°F (787°C to 843°C) and holding for 10-15 minutes before annealing and cooling.

Cooling and Finishing: Allow the kiln to cool to room temperature before removing your coasters. Remove any residue with water and a soft cloth. Your fused glass coasters are now ready for use!

Fused Glass Pendant

Materials Needed:

- Sheet glass (compatible COE)
- Glass cutter
- Running pliers
- Kiln and kiln shelf
- Kiln wash or kiln paper
- Jewelry bails or findings
- Safety gear (glasses, gloves, mask)
- Optional: Glass frit, stringers, or dichroic glass for decoration

Steps:

Design: Sketch out a simple design for your pendant. Popular shapes include rectangles, circles, or freeform organic shapes.

Prepare Glass: Cut your sheet glass into the desired shape for your pendant using a glass cutter. You can also add decorative elements like frit, stringers, or dichroic glass to enhance your design.

Attach Bail: Place a jewelry bail or finding on the back of your glass pendant, ensuring it is centered and securely attached.

Fire Kiln: Place your pendant on a kiln shelf lined with kiln wash or paper. Program your kiln with a tack fusing schedule appropriate for the thickness of your glass and any added decorations.

Cooling and Finishing: Once the kiln has cooled to room temperature, remove your pendant and attach a necklace chain or cord. Clean any residue from the glass with water and a soft cloth. Your fused glass pendant is now ready to wear or gift!

Fused Glass Sun Catcher

Materials Needed:

- Sheet glass (compatible COE)
- Glass cutter
- Running pliers
- Kiln and kiln shelf
- Kiln wash or kiln paper
- Safety gear (glasses, gloves, mask)
- Glass stringers or frit for decoration
- Copper foil tape or wire for hanging

Steps:

Design: Choose a simple shape for your sun catcher, such as a flower, butterfly, or geometric design. Sketch out your design on paper or directly on the glass.

Prepare Glass: Cut your sheet glass into the desired shape using a glass cutter. You can also use glass stringers or frit to add decorative elements to your design.

Assemble: Arrange your glass pieces on the kiln shelf, ensuring they are spaced apart to allow for proper fusing. If desired, use copper foil tape or wire to create a loop for hanging.

Fire Kiln: Program your kiln with a tack fusing schedule suitable for the thickness of your glass. This typically involves a ramp-up to around 1300°F (704°C) and a short hold before annealing and cooling.

Cooling and Finishing: Once the kiln has cooled to room temperature, remove your sun catcher and attach a suction cup or wire for hanging. Clean any residue from the glass with water and a soft cloth. Your fused glass sun catcher is now ready to brighten up your window!

Fused Glass Magnets

Materials Needed:

- Sheet glass (compatible COE)
- Glass cutter
- Running pliers
- Kiln and kiln shelf
- Kiln wash or kiln paper
- Safety gear (glasses, gloves, mask)
- Magnets
- Glass stringers or frit for decoration

Steps:

Design: Decide on the size and shape of your magnets. Rectangles, squares, or circles work well for this project. Sketch out your design on paper or directly on the glass.

Prepare Glass: Cut your sheet glass into the desired shapes using a glass cutter. You can also use glass stringers or frit to add decorative accents to your magnets.

Assemble: Arrange your glass pieces on the kiln shelf, leaving a small space between each magnet. Place a magnet on the back of each glass piece.

Fire Kiln: Program your kiln with a tack fusing schedule suitable for the thickness of your glass. This typically involves a ramp-up to around 1300°F (704°C) and a short hold before annealing and cooling.

Cooling and Finishing: Once the kiln has cooled to room temperature, remove your glass magnets. Clean any residue from the glass with water and a soft cloth. Your fused glass magnets are now ready to adorn your fridge or magnetic board!

Fused Glass Dish

Materials Needed:

- Sheet glass (compatible COE)
- Glass cutter
- Running pliers
- Kiln and kiln shelf
- Kiln wash or kiln paper
- Safety gear (glasses, gloves, mask)
- Glass frit, stringers, or noodles for decoration
- Optional: Glass slumping mold

Steps:

Design: Decide on the shape and size of your dish. Simple shapes like squares, circles, or rectangles work well for beginners. Sketch out your design on paper or directly on the glass.

Prepare Glass: Cut your sheet glass into the desired shape using a glass cutter. You can also experiment with adding decorative elements like frit, stringers, or noodles to your design.

Assemble: Arrange your glass pieces on the kiln shelf, ensuring they are spaced apart to allow for proper fusing. If desired, place the glass on a slumping mold to give it a curved shape.

Fire Kiln: Program your kiln with a full fusing schedule suitable for the thickness of your glass. This typically involves a ramp-up to around 1450°F to 1550°F (787°C to 843°C) and a hold before annealing and cooling.

Cooling and Finishing: Once the kiln has cooled to room temperature, remove your fused glass dish. Clean any residue from the glass with water and a soft cloth. Your fused glass dish is now ready to use for serving snacks, holding jewelry, or as a decorative accent!

Fused Glass Wall Art

Materials Needed:

- Sheet glass (compatible COE)
- Glass cutter
- Running pliers
- Kiln and kiln shelf
- Kiln wash or kiln paper
- Safety gear (glasses, gloves, mask)
- Glass frit, stringers, or noodles for decoration
- Optional: Glass slump mold, metal standoffs for mounting

Steps:

Design: Sketch out your design on paper, considering the size and shape of your wall art. Abstract patterns, landscapes, or geometric designs are great for beginners.

Prepare Glass: Cut your sheet glass into the desired shapes for your design using a glass cutter. You can also experiment with layering different colors and adding decorative elements like frit or stringers.

Assemble: Arrange your glass pieces on the kiln shelf, layering them to create your design. If desired, use a slump mold to give your wall art a three-dimensional shape.

Fire Kiln: Program your kiln with a full fusing schedule suitable for the thickness of your glass. This typically involves a ramp-up to around 1450°F to 1550°F (787°C to 843°C) and a hold before annealing and cooling.

Mounting: Once the kiln has cooled to room temperature, mount your fused glass wall art using metal standoffs or other mounting hardware. Clean any residue from the glass with water and a soft cloth. Your fused glass wall art is now ready to hang and showcase in your home or office!

CHAPTER 6
Intermediate Projects

Fused Glass Bowl with Inclusions

Materials Needed:

- Sheet glass (compatible COE)
- Glass cutter
- Running pliers
- Kiln and kiln shelf
- Kiln wash or kiln paper
- Safety gear (glasses, gloves, mask)
- Glass frit, stringers, or noodles for decoration
- Inclusion materials (such as metal wires, foils, or glass beads)
- Glass slumping mold

Steps:

Design: Decide on the size and shape of your bowl. Sketch out your design on paper, considering the incorporation of inclusion materials for added texture and visual interest.

Prepare Glass: Cut your sheet glass into the desired shape for the base of your bowl using a glass cutter. Cut additional pieces for the sides of the bowl, allowing for overlap and thickness.

Add Inclusions: Arrange metal wires, foils, or glass beads on the base layer of glass, taking care to distribute them evenly and create an appealing design.

Assemble: Layer the additional pieces of glass for the sides of the bowl on top of the base layer, ensuring they overlap and fuse together securely.

Decorate: Sprinkle glass frit, stringers, or noodles on top of the assembled glass layers to add color and decoration to your bowl.

Fire Kiln: Program your kiln with a full fusing schedule suitable for the thickness of your glass. This typically involves a ramp-up to around 1450°F to 1550°F (787°C to 843°C) and a hold before annealing and cooling.

Slumping: Once the fused glass has cooled to room temperature, place it on a glass slumping mold and fire the kiln again to slump the glass into the desired bowl shape.

Cooling and Finishing: Allow the kiln to cool to room temperature before removing your fused glass bowl. Clean any residue from the glass with water and a soft cloth. Your fused glass bowl with inclusions is now ready to use as a decorative centerpiece or serving dish!

Fused Glass Mosaic Panel

Materials Needed:

- Sheet glass (compatible COE)
- Glass cutter
- Running pliers
- Kiln and kiln shelf
- Kiln wash or kiln paper
- Safety gear (glasses, gloves, mask)
- Glass frit, stringers, or noodles for decoration
- Grout
- Mosaic backing material (such as wood or cement board)

Steps:

Design: Sketch out your design on paper, considering the size and shape of your mosaic panel. Abstract patterns, landscapes, or geometric designs are great options for mosaic projects.

Prepare Glass: Cut your sheet glass into small pieces using a glass cutter, creating a variety of shapes and sizes for your mosaic design. You can also use glass frit, stringers, or noodles to add texture and detail to your mosaic.

Assemble: Arrange your glass pieces on the mosaic backing material, adhering them with glue or mortar to create your desired design. Leave small gaps between the glass pieces to allow for grouting later.

Decorate: Sprinkle glass frit, stringers, or noodles on top of the assembled glass pieces to add color and texture to your mosaic design.

Fire Kiln: Program your kiln with a tack fusing schedule suitable for the thickness of your glass. This typically involves a ramp-up to around 1300°F to 1350°F (704°C to 732°C) and a short hold before annealing and cooling.

Grouting: Once the fused glass has cooled to room temperature, apply grout between the glass pieces using a rubber float, pressing it into the gaps and smoothing it over the surface.

Cleaning: Allow the grout to dry according to the manufacturer's instructions, then wipe away any excess grout from the surface of the glass with a damp sponge.

Finishing: Once the grout has fully dried, clean the surface of the glass with a soft cloth and glass cleaner to remove any remaining residue. Your fused glass mosaic panel is now ready to display as a stunning piece of art!

Fused Glass Vase

Materials Needed:

- Sheet glass (compatible COE)
- Glass cutter
- Running pliers
- Kiln and kiln shelf
- Kiln wash or kiln paper
- Safety gear (glasses, gloves, mask)
- Glass frit, stringers, or noodles for decoration
- Glass slumping mold

Steps:

Design: Decide on the size and shape of your vase. Sketch out your design on paper, considering the incorporation of decorative elements like frit, stringers, or noodles.

Prepare Glass: Cut your sheet glass into the desired shapes for the sides of your vase using a glass cutter. Create additional pieces for the base and lip of the vase, ensuring they fit together securely.

Assemble: Arrange the glass pieces for the sides of the vase on a kiln shelf, overlapping them slightly to create a seamless design. Add decorative elements like frit, stringers, or noodles between the glass pieces as desired.

Fire Kiln: Program your kiln with a full fusing schedule suitable for the thickness of your glass. This typically involves a ramp-up to around 1450°F to 1550°F (787°C to 843°C) and a hold before annealing and cooling.

Slumping: Once the fused glass has cooled to room temperature, place it on a glass slumping mold and fire the kiln again to slump the glass into the desired vase shape.

Cooling and Finishing: Allow the kiln to cool to room temperature before removing your fused glass vase. Clean any residue from the glass with water and a soft cloth. Your fused glass vase is now ready to display with fresh flowers or as a standalone art piece!

Fused Glass Wall Clock

Materials Needed:

- Sheet glass (compatible COE)
- Glass cutter
- Running pliers
- Kiln and kiln shelf
- Kiln wash or kiln paper
- Safety gear (glasses, gloves, mask)
- Clock mechanism and hands
- Glass frit, stringers, or noodles for decoration

Steps:

Design: Sketch out your design on paper, considering the size and shape of your wall clock. Popular designs include geometric patterns, abstract shapes, or nature-inspired motifs.

Prepare Glass: Cut your sheet glass into the desired shapes for your clock face and any decorative elements using a glass cutter. Create additional pieces for the numbers or markers on the clock face.

Assemble: Arrange the glass pieces for the clock face on a kiln shelf, layering them to create your design. Add decorative elements like frit, stringers, or noodles between the glass pieces as desired.

Attach Clock Mechanism: Once the fused glass has cooled to room temperature, drill a hole in the center of the clock face and attach the clock mechanism according to the manufacturer's instructions.

Fire Kiln: Program your kiln with a tack fusing schedule suitable for the thickness of your glass. This typically involves a ramp-up to around 1300°F to 1350°F (704°C to 732°C) and a short hold before annealing and cooling.

Finishing: Once the fused glass has cooled completely, attach the clock hands to the clock mechanism. Hang your fused glass wall clock on the wall using a sturdy hook or mounting hardware. Enjoy your handmade clock as a functional and stylish piece of art in your home or office!

CHAPTER 7
Advanced Projects

Fused Glass Sculpture

Materials Needed:

- Sheet glass (compatible COE)
- Glass cutter
- Running pliers
- Kiln and kiln shelf
- Kiln wash or kiln paper
- Safety gear (glasses, gloves, mask)
- Glass frit, stringers, or noodles for decoration
- Sculpting tools (such as diamond bits or abrasive wheels)

- Glass casting mold or kiln carving materials (optional)

Steps:

Design: Sketch out your sculpture design on paper, considering the size, shape, and overall composition. Decide on any specific features or details you want to incorporate into your sculpture.

Prepare Glass: Cut your sheet glass into the desired shapes for the various components of your sculpture using a glass cutter. You can also use glass frit, stringers, or noodles to add texture and detail to your design.

Assemble: Arrange the glass pieces on a kiln shelf, layering them and fusing them together to create the structure of your sculpture. Use sculpting tools to carve and shape the glass as needed to achieve your desired form.

Decorate: Add additional layers of glass frit, stringers, or noodles to enhance the texture and detail of your sculpture. Try out various colors and opacities to add visual intrigue.

Fire Kiln: Program your kiln with a full fusing schedule suitable for the thickness of your glass. This typically involves a ramp-up to around 1450°F to 1550°F (787°C to 843°C) and a hold before annealing and cooling.

Finishing: Once the fused glass has cooled to room temperature, remove your sculpture from the kiln and inspect it for any rough edges or imperfections. Use grinding tools or abrasive wheels to smooth and polish the surface as needed. Your fused glass sculpture is now ready to display as a stunning piece of art!

Fused Glass Installation

Materials Needed:

- Sheet glass (compatible COE)
- Glass cutter
- Running pliers
- Kiln and kiln shelf
- Kiln wash or kiln paper
- Safety gear (glasses, gloves, mask)
- Glass frit, stringers, or noodles for decoration
- Metal framework or mounting hardware
- Installation site and tools (if applicable)

Steps:

Design: Collaborate with a client or create a concept for your fused glass installation, considering the size, shape, and location of the piece. Sketch out your design on paper or use digital rendering software to visualize the project.

Prepare Glass: Cut your sheet glass into the desired shapes and sizes for the various components of your installation using a glass cutter. Consider incorporating layers, textures, and colors to enhance the visual impact of the piece.

Assemble: Arrange the glass pieces on a kiln shelf, layering them and fusing them together to create the individual elements of your installation. Use glass frit, stringers, or noodles to add detail and depth to your design.

Decorate: Experiment with different techniques, such as glass printing, kiln carving, or glass casting, to create unique effects and textures in your installation. Incorporate additional materials like metal or wood to complement the fused glass components.

Fire Kiln: Program your kiln with a full fusing schedule suitable for the thickness of your glass. This typically involves a ramp-up to around 1450°F to 1550°F (787°C to 843°C) and a hold before annealing and cooling.

Installation: Once the fused glass has cooled to room temperature, carefully transport and install your installation at the designated site. Use metal framework or mounting hardware to secure the glass components in place and ensure stability and safety.

Finishing: Inspect the installation for any adjustments or touch-ups needed, such as cleaning or polishing the glass surfaces. Your fused glass installation is now ready to be admired and enjoyed as a captivating and enduring piece of public or private art!

Fused Glass Mural

Materials Needed:

- Sheet glass (compatible COE)
- Glass cutter
- Running pliers
- Kiln and kiln shelf
- Kiln wash or kiln paper
- Safety gear (glasses, gloves, mask)

- Glass frit, stringers, or noodles for decoration
- Mural backing material (such as metal, wood, or glass)
- Installation tools and materials (if applicable)

Steps:

Design: Plan out your mural design, considering the size, theme, and location for installation. Sketch out your design on paper or use digital rendering software for precision.

Prepare Glass: Cut your sheet glass into various shapes and sizes to create the elements of your mural using a glass cutter. Consider incorporating layers, textures, and colors to enhance the visual impact of the piece.

Assemble: Arrange the glass pieces on a kiln shelf, layering them and fusing them together to create the composition of your mural. Use glass frit, stringers, or noodles to add detail and depth to your design.

Decorate: Experiment with advanced techniques like glass powder printing, kiln carving, or glass casting to create unique effects and textures in your mural. Incorporate additional materials like metal or ceramic elements for added dimension.

Fire Kiln: Program your kiln with a full fusing schedule suitable for the thickness of your glass. This typically involves a ramp-up to around 1450°F to 1550°F (787°C to 843°C) and a hold before annealing and cooling.

Installation: Once the fused glass has cooled to room temperature, carefully transport and install your mural at the designated site. Use appropriate installation tools and materials to secure the glass components in place and ensure stability and safety.

Finishing: Inspect the mural for any adjustments or touch-ups needed, such as cleaning or polishing the glass surfaces. Your fused glass mural is now ready to be admired and enjoyed as a striking and enduring piece of art!

Fused Glass Functional Art Furniture

Materials Needed:

- Sheet glass (compatible COE)
- Glass cutter
- Running pliers
- Kiln and kiln shelf
- Kiln wash or kiln paper
- Safety gear (glasses, gloves, mask)
- Glass frit, stringers, or noodles for decoration
- Furniture frame or base (such as metal, wood, or acrylic)

Steps:

Design: Conceptualize your functional art furniture piece, considering the form, function, and integration of fused glass elements. Sketch out your design on paper or use digital rendering software for precision.

Prepare Glass: Cut your sheet glass into various shapes and sizes to create the fused glass components of your furniture piece using a glass cutter. Experiment with different colors, textures, and techniques to achieve your desired aesthetic.

Assemble: Arrange the glass pieces on a kiln shelf, layering them and fusing them together to create the decorative elements of your furniture. Use glass frit, stringers, or noodles to add detail and interest to your design.

Integrate with Furniture Frame: Once the fused glass components have cooled to room temperature, carefully integrate them into the furniture frame or base using appropriate adhesives or mounting hardware. Ensure that the glass components are securely attached and supported.

Fire Kiln: Program your kiln with a full fusing schedule suitable for the thickness of your glass. This typically involves a ramp-up to around 1450°F to 1550°F (787°C to

843°C) and a hold before annealing and cooling.

Finishing: Inspect the furniture piece for any adjustments or touch-ups needed, such as cleaning or polishing the glass surfaces. Your fused glass functional art furniture is now ready to be showcased and appreciated as a stunning and functional work of art!

Fused Glass Sculptural Lighting Fixture

Materials Needed:

- Sheet glass (compatible COE)
- Glass cutter
- Running pliers

- Kiln and kiln shelf
- Kiln wash or kiln paper
- Safety gear (glasses, gloves, mask)
- Glass frit, stringers, or noodles for decoration
- Lighting fixture components (such as lampshade frame, LED lights, wiring)
- Sculpting tools (such as diamond bits or abrasive wheels)

Steps:

Design: Sketch out your lighting fixture design, considering the size, shape, and overall aesthetic. Determine how the fused glass components will interact with light and shadow to create dynamic visual effects.

Prepare Glass: Cut your sheet glass into various shapes and sizes to create the fused glass components of your lighting fixture using a glass cutter. Experiment with different colors, textures, and opacities to achieve your desired lighting effects.

Assemble: Arrange the glass pieces on a kiln shelf, layering them and fusing them together to create the sculptural elements of your lighting fixture. Use sculpting tools to shape and texture the glass as desired.

Decorate: Add additional layers of glass frit, stringers, or noodles to enhance the texture and visual interest of your sculpture. Consider incorporating elements that will interact with light, such as dichroic glass or iridescent coatings.

Fire Kiln: Program your kiln with a full fusing schedule suitable for the thickness of your glass. This typically involves a ramp-up to around 1450°F to 1550°F (787°C to 843°C) and a hold before annealing and cooling.

Integrate with Lighting Fixture: Once the fused glass components have cooled to room temperature, carefully integrate them into the lighting fixture frame or base. Ensure that the glass components are securely attached and will interact with the light source as intended.

Testing: Test the functionality of the lighting fixture, ensuring that it produces the desired lighting effects and distributes light evenly. Make any necessary adjustments to the positioning or configuration of the glass components.

Finishing: Inspect the lighting fixture for any adjustments or touch-ups needed, such as cleaning or polishing the glass surfaces. Your fused glass sculptural lighting fixture is now ready to illuminate and enhance any space with its unique beauty and artistic flair!

Fused Glass Architectural Feature

Materials Needed:

- Sheet glass (compatible COE)
- Glass cutter
- Running pliers

- Kiln and kiln shelf
- Kiln wash or kiln paper
- Safety gear (glasses, gloves, mask)
- Glass frit, stringers, or noodles for decoration
- Architectural framework or base (such as metal, wood, or concrete)
- Installation tools and materials (if applicable)

Steps:

Design: Collaborate with architects or designers to conceptualize an architectural feature incorporating fused glass elements. Consider the scale, location, and function of the feature within the space.

Prepare Glass: Cut your sheet glass into various shapes and sizes to create the fused glass components of the architectural feature using a glass cutter. Experiment with different colors, textures, and patterns to complement the overall design.

Assemble: Arrange the glass pieces on a kiln shelf, layering them and fusing them together to create the structural and decorative elements of the architectural feature. Consider how natural light will interact with the glass to create visual interest and ambiance.

Decorate: Add additional layers of glass frit, stringers, or noodles to enhance the texture and visual impact of your architectural feature. Incorporate elements that reflect the surrounding environment or evoke a specific mood or theme.

Fire Kiln: Program your kiln with a full fusing schedule suitable for the thickness of your glass. This typically involves a ramp-up to around 1450°F to 1550°F (787°C to 843°C) and a hold before annealing and cooling.

Integrate with Architecture: Once the fused glass components have cooled to room temperature, carefully integrate them into the architectural framework or base. Ensure that the glass components are securely attached and will withstand environmental conditions.

Installation: Coordinate with construction teams or installation specialists to transport and install the architectural feature at the designated site. Use appropriate tools and materials to secure the feature in place and ensure its stability and longevity.

Finishing: Inspect the architectural feature for any adjustments or touch-ups needed, such as cleaning or polishing the glass surfaces. Your fused glass architectural feature is now ready to enhance and elevate the aesthetic of any space with its striking beauty and craftsmanship!

CHAPTER 8
Troubleshooting and Tips

Troubleshooting in fused glass making can be crucial for achieving desired results.

Cracking or Breaking During Firing:

Possible Causes: Rapid temperature changes, uneven thickness of glass, or incompatible glass types.

Solutions:

Ensure a slow and controlled ramp-up and ramp-down cycle in your kiln to prevent thermal shock.

Use glass of uniform thickness throughout your project.

Ensure all glass used in a project is compatible with each other in terms of coefficient of expansion (COE).

Bubbles or Devitrification on the Surface:

Possible Causes: Contaminants on the glass surface, improper cleaning, or firing at too high a temperature.

Solutions:

Clean glass thoroughly before firing to remove any contaminants.

Use a cleaner firing schedule with a slower ramp-up and hold to prevent devitrification.

Consider using a devitrification spray or coating to prevent surface issues.

Uneven Heating or Hot Spots:

Possible Causes: Poor kiln ventilation, uneven distribution of glass in the kiln, or kiln shelves in need of leveling.

Solutions:

Ensure proper kiln ventilation to promote even heat distribution.

Arrange glass pieces evenly on the kiln shelf, avoiding overcrowding.

Check and level kiln shelves regularly to prevent hot spots.

Glass Sticking to Kiln Shelf:

Possible Causes: Insufficient kiln wash or kiln paper, or firing at too high a temperature.

Solutions:

Apply a fresh coat of kiln wash or use new kiln paper before each firing.

Ensure firing temperatures are within the recommended range for the type of glass and project.

Warping or Slumping Irregularities:

Possible Causes: Uneven heating, inadequate support for glass during slumping, or improper kiln programming.

Solutions:

Ensure even heating by placing slumping molds or supports under glass pieces during slumping.

Use proper kiln programming for slumping, including appropriate ramp-up, hold, and cooling schedules.

Color Changes or Loss of Detail:

Possible Causes: Firing at too high a temperature or for too long, or incompatible glass types.

Solutions:

Follow recommended firing schedules provided by the glass manufacturer.

Choose compatible glass types and colors for your projects to avoid color changes or loss of detail.

Over-Firing or Under-Firing:

Possible Causes: Incorrect programming of the kiln, inaccurate temperature measurement, or outdated kiln elements.

Solutions:

Double-check kiln programming to ensure it matches the recommended firing schedule.

Use a pyrometer or kiln controller to monitor and adjust firing temperatures as needed.

Replace kiln elements if they are old or damaged to ensure consistent heating.

General Tips

Start Small: Begin with simple projects and techniques before progressing to more complex ones. This will help you build confidence and skills gradually.

Use Compatible Glass: Ensure that all glass used in a project has the same coefficient of expansion (COE) to prevent cracking or breaking during firing. Check compatibility charts provided by glass manufacturers.

Proper Cutting: Use a glass cutter and running pliers to score and break glass accurately. Practice cutting straight lines and curves to achieve clean edges.

Cleanliness is Key: Thoroughly clean glass pieces before firing to remove any dirt, oil, or contaminants that could affect the final result. Use a gentle detergent with water, and rinse thoroughly afterward.

Experiment with Design: Don't be afraid to experiment with different colors, textures, and techniques to create unique and interesting designs. Sketch out your ideas beforehand to plan your project effectively.

Ventilation: Ensure proper ventilation in your workspace, especially when firing glass in a kiln. Ventilation helps to remove fumes and prevents the buildup of harmful gases.

Safety First: Always wear appropriate safety gear, including safety glasses, gloves, and a mask, when cutting or handling glass. Follow safety guidelines provided by equipment manufacturers and glass suppliers.

Keep Records: Keep detailed records of your firing schedules, including temperature ramps, hold times, and cooling cycles. This will help you replicate successful results and troubleshoot issues if they arise.

Practice Patience: Fused glass making requires patience and attention to detail. Allow sufficient time for glass to cool properly between firings and avoid rushing the process.

Learn from mistakes: Don't let setbacks discourage you. Instead, view them as valuable learning opportunities. Analyze what went wrong, adjust your approach, and grow from the experience.

Join a Community: Consider joining a local glass fusing group or online community to connect with other glass artists, share ideas, and learn from each other's experiences.

Have Fun: Most importantly, have fun with your fused glass making! Enjoy the creative process and the satisfaction of bringing your ideas to life in glass.

CONCLUSION

Fused glass making is a fascinating and rewarding art form that offers endless opportunities for creativity and expression. From beginner projects to advanced techniques, there's always something new to learn and explore in the world of fused glass.

Throughout this book, we've covered the history, techniques, materials, tools, safety precautions, and troubleshooting tips necessary for success in fused glass making. We've delved into the art and craft of fused glass, explored its therapeutic benefits, and provided step-by-step instructions for a variety of projects at different skill levels.

Whether you're a beginner just starting out or an experienced artist looking to expand your skills, I hope this book has inspired and encouraged you on your fused glass journey. Remember to practice patience, embrace experimentation, and always prioritize safety in your work.

As you continue to explore the possibilities of fused glass, don't forget to have fun and enjoy the creative process. Let your imagination soar and see where it takes you in the vibrant and dynamic world of fused glass art.

Thank you for joining me on this journey, and may your fused glass adventures be filled with joy, inspiration, and endless possibilities.

Made in United States
North Haven, CT
21 July 2024